13 Words Halloween
Coloring Book For Kids
(Dover Holiday Coloring Books)

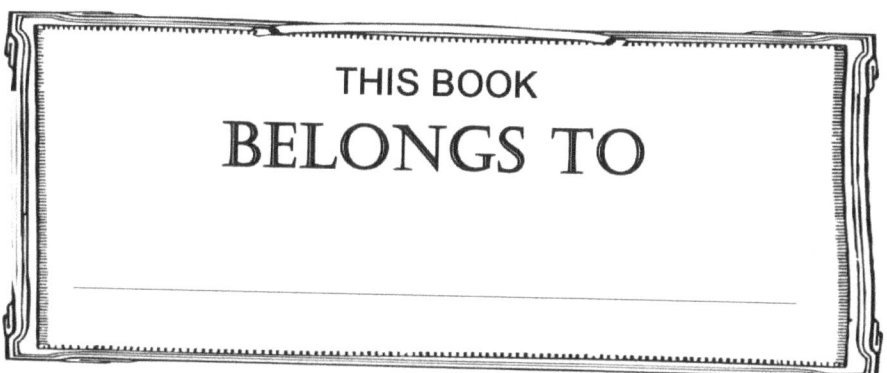

Copyrighted Material

All rights reserved. No part of this publication may be reproduced, stored in retrieval system, copied in any form or by any means, electronic, mechanical, photocopying, recording or otherwise transmitted without written permission from the publisher.

Travis T. Johnson

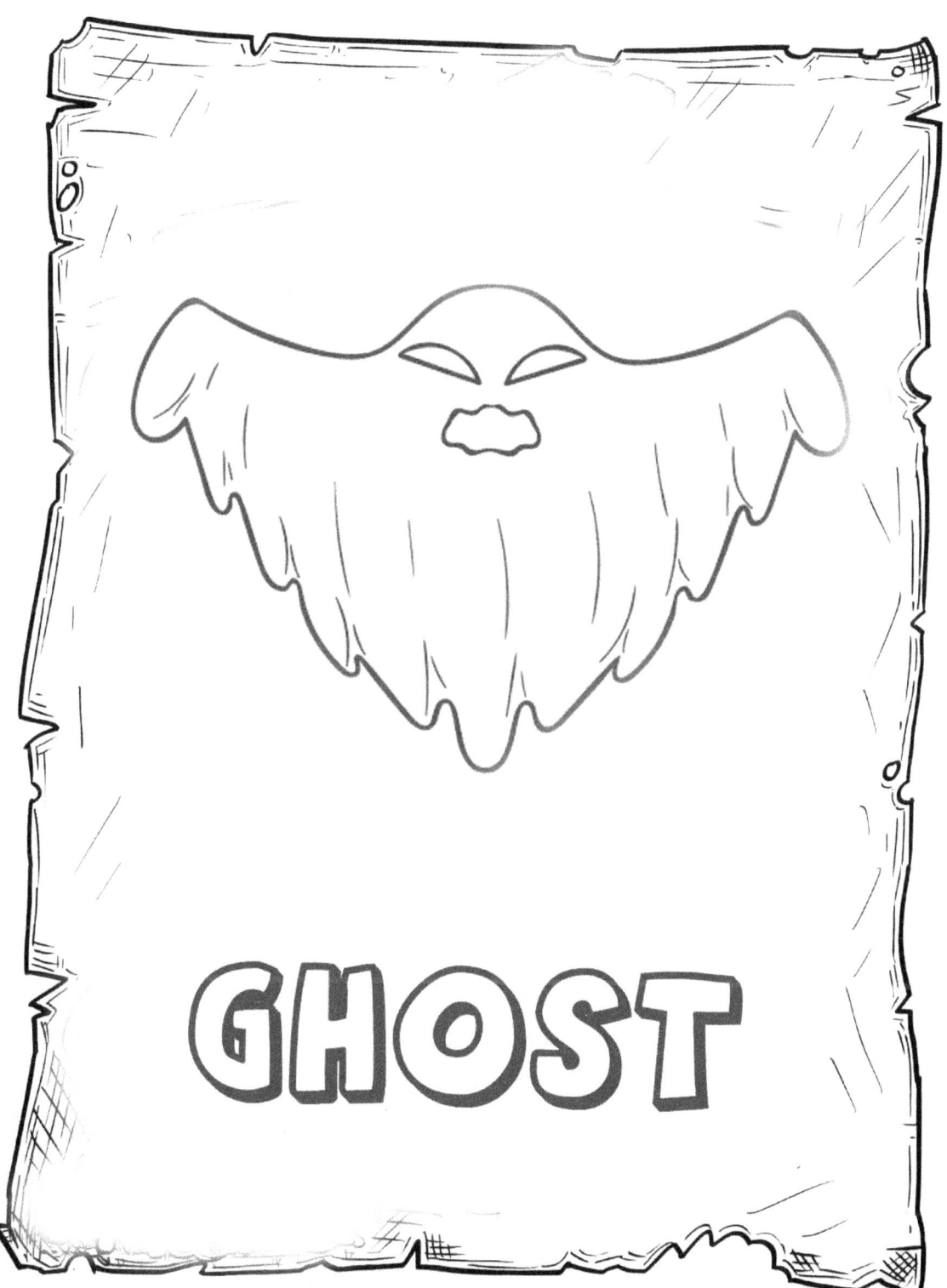

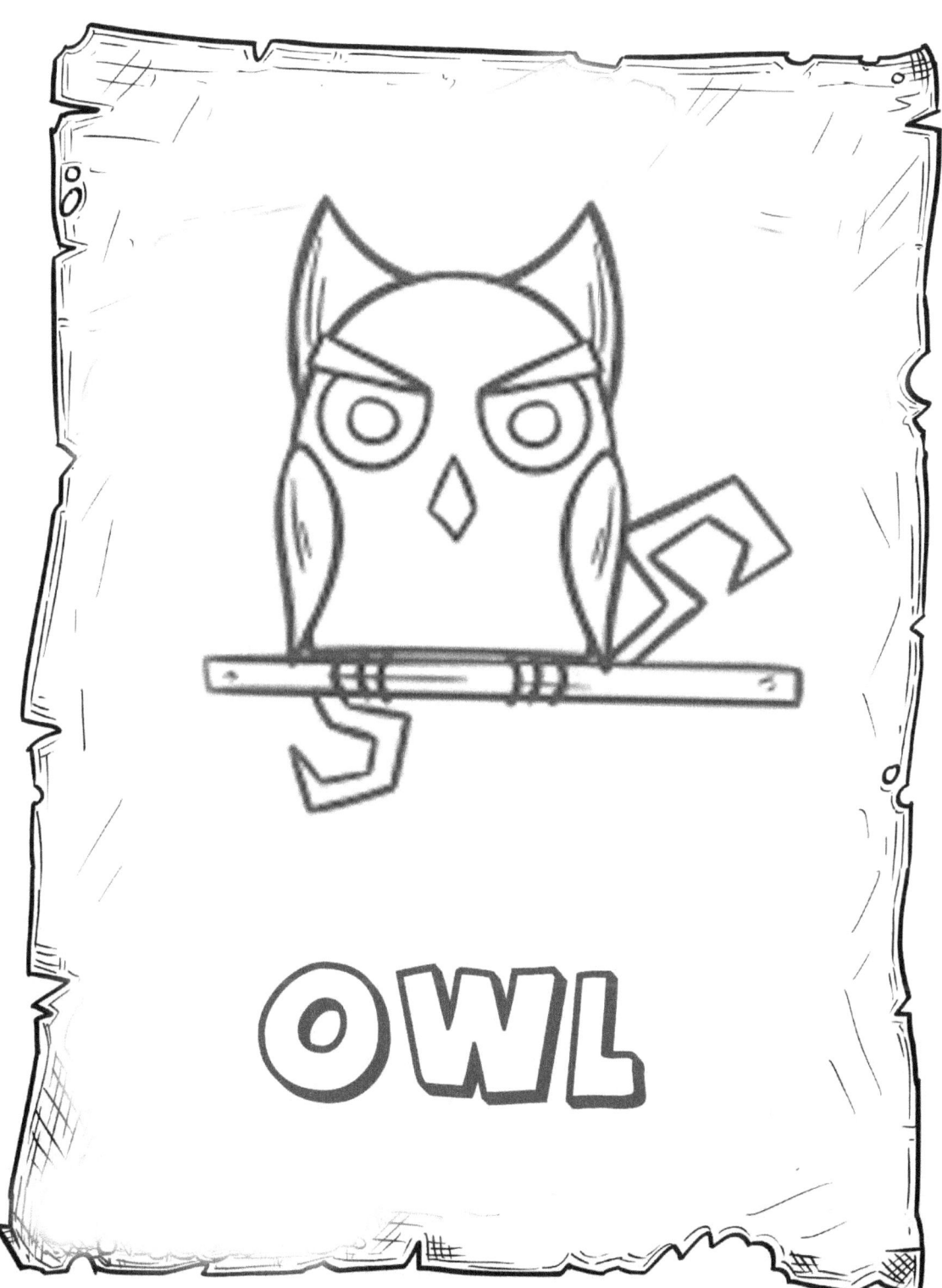

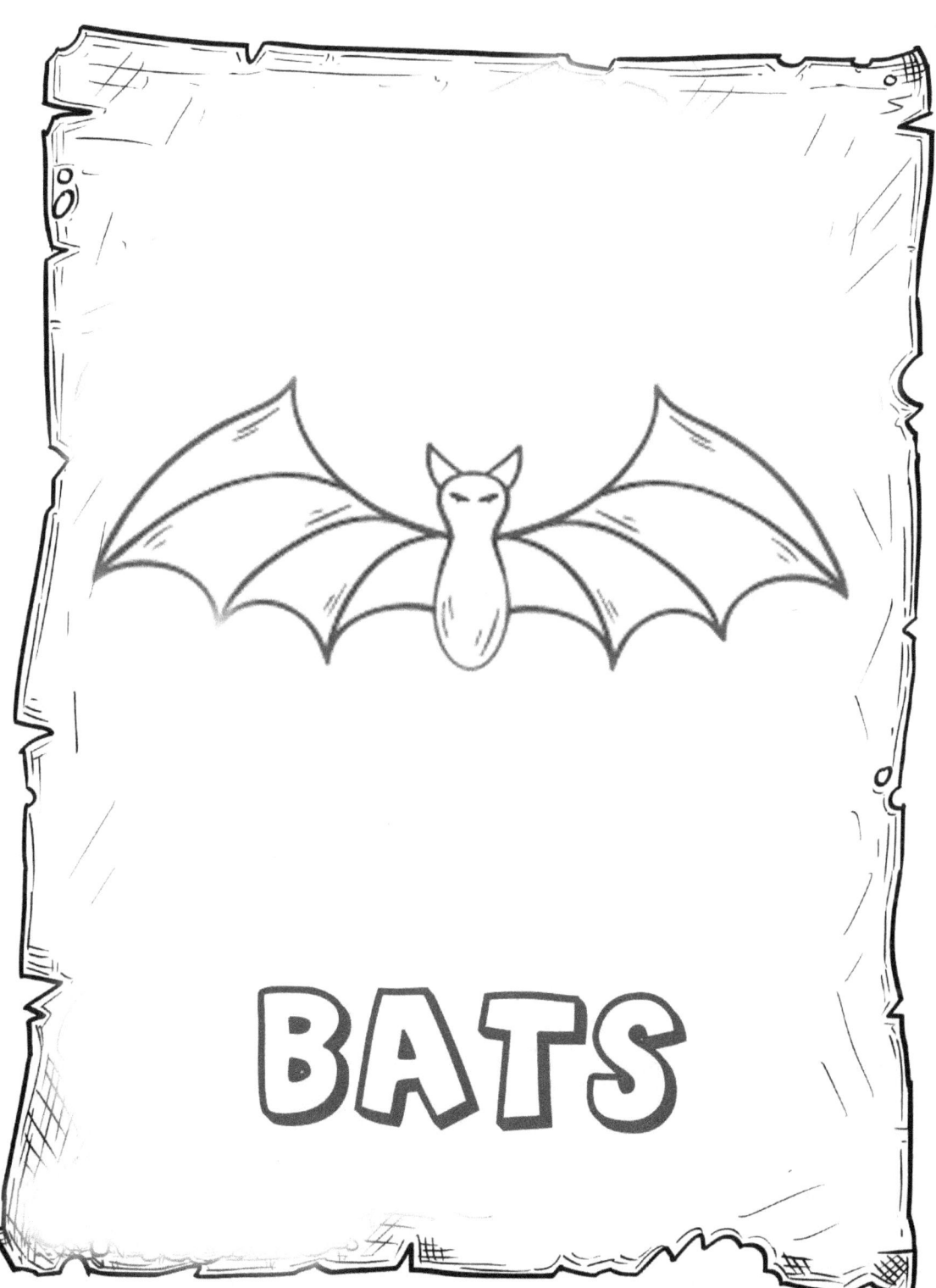

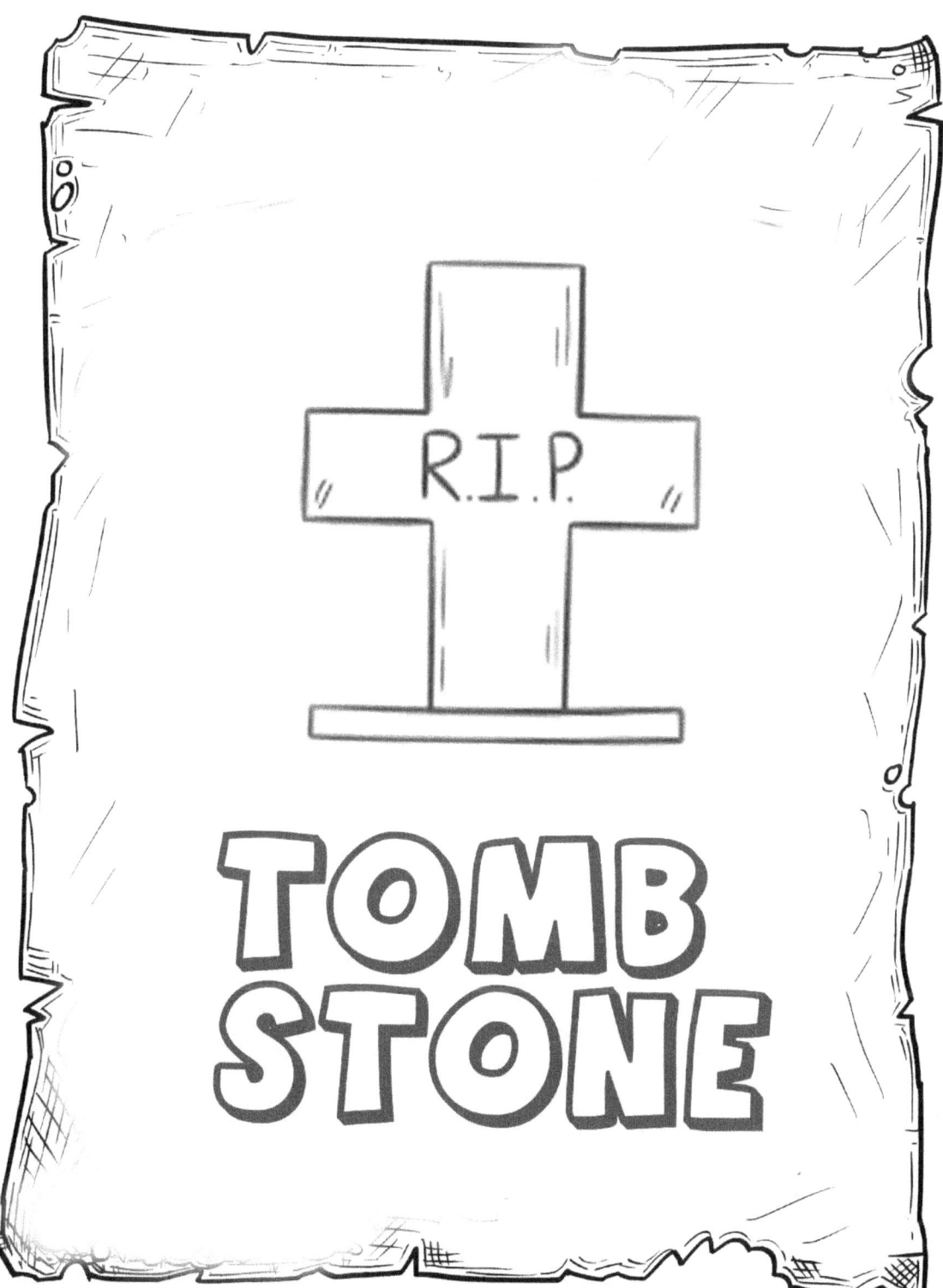

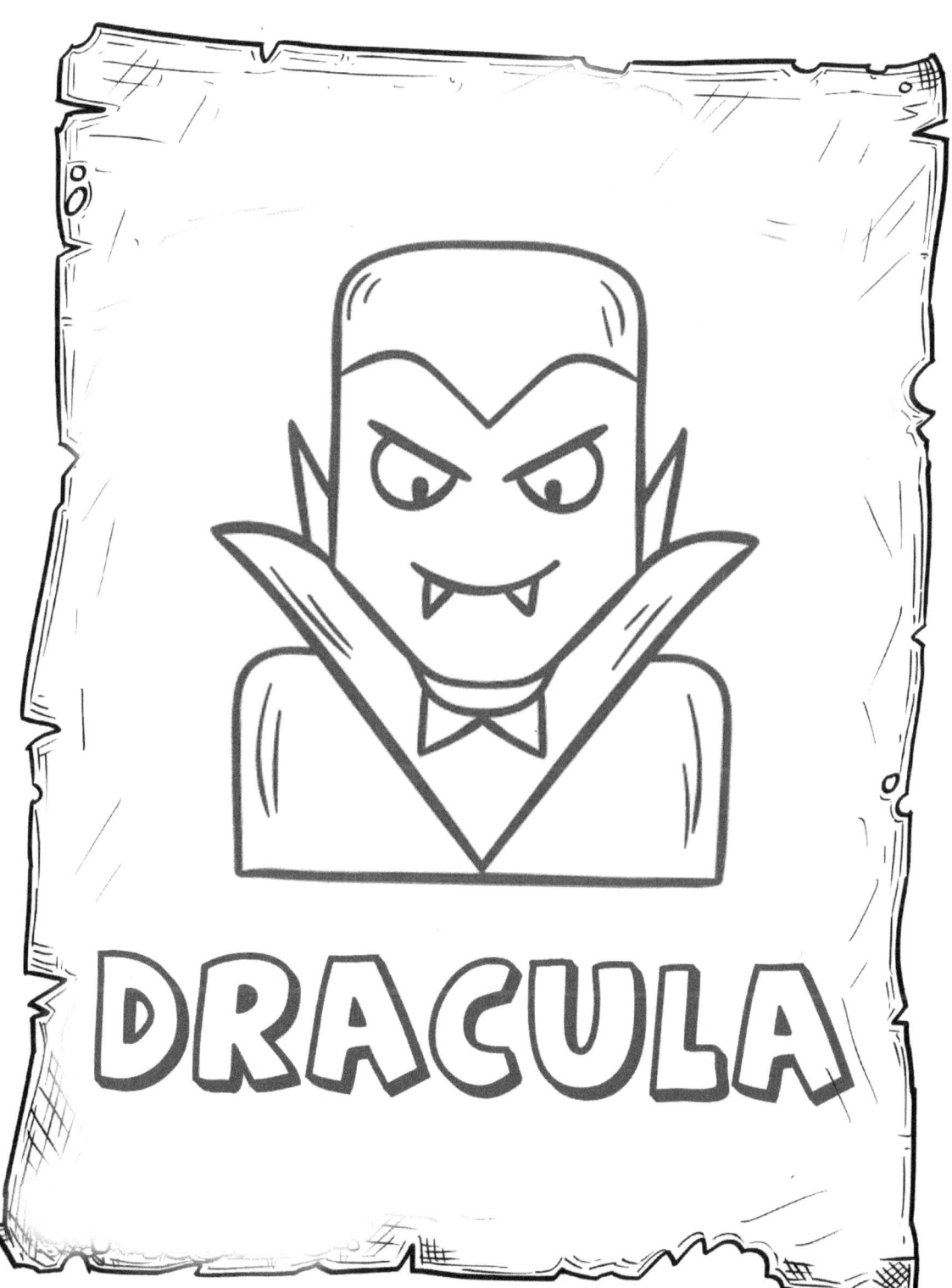

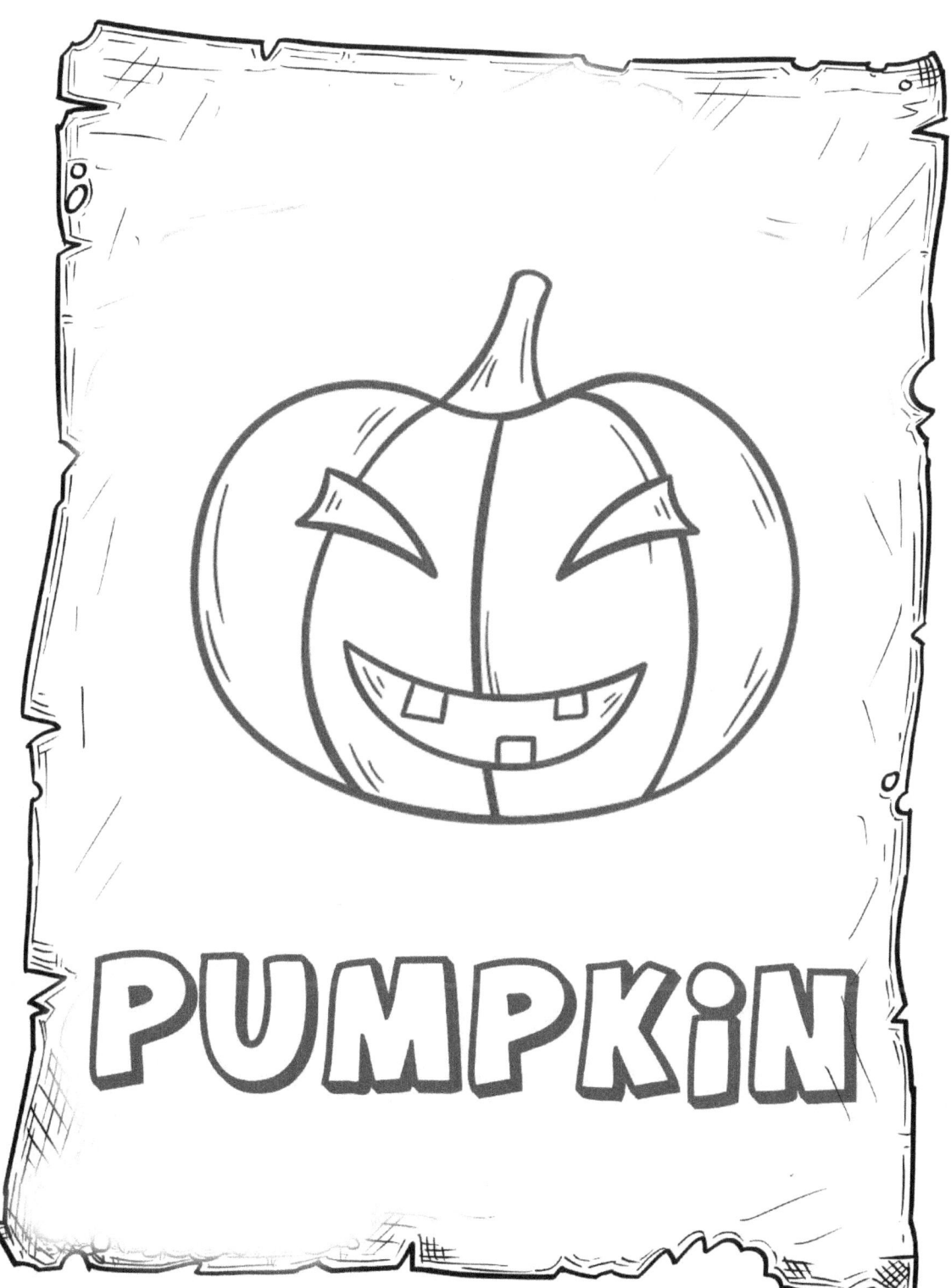

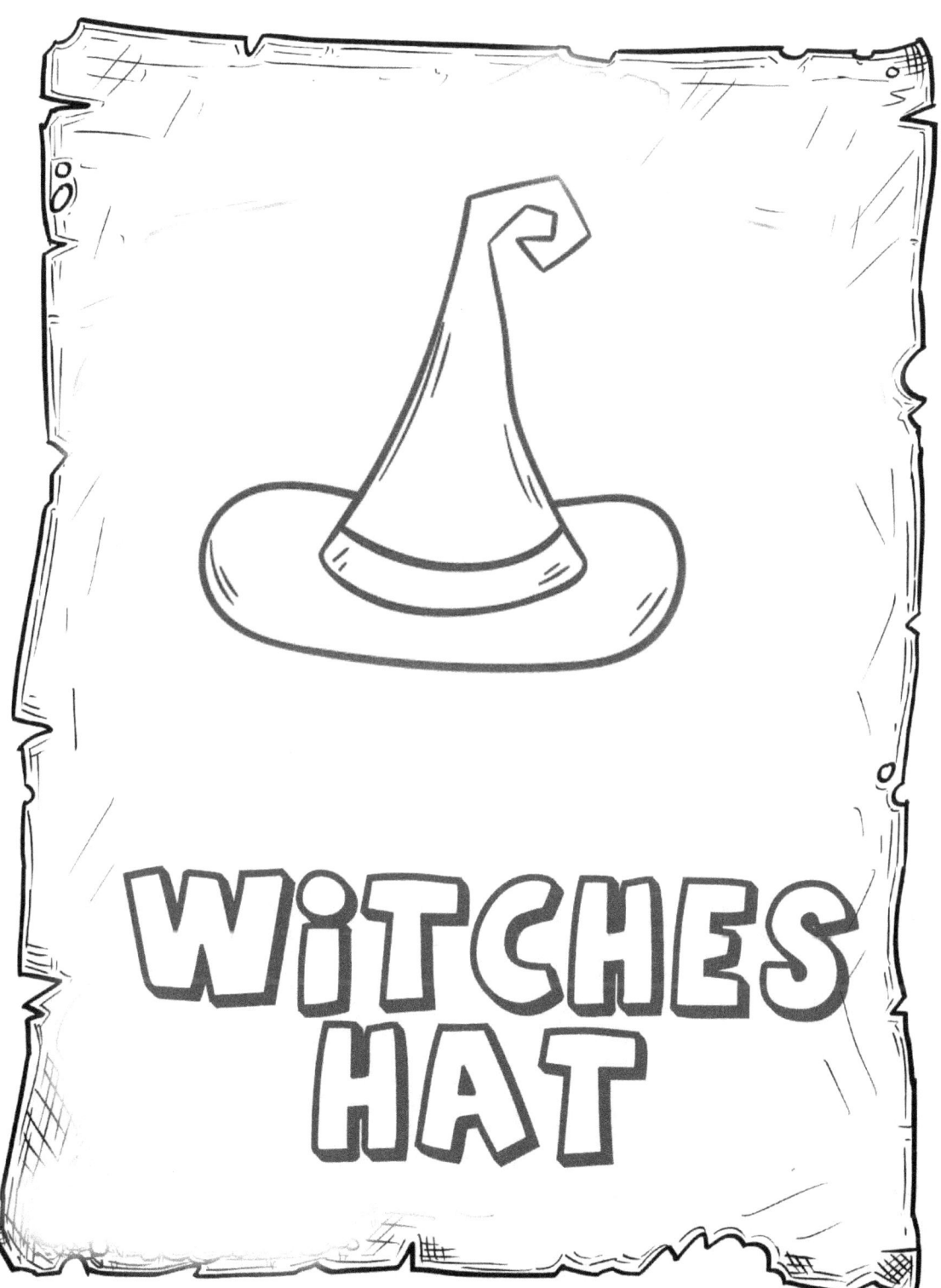

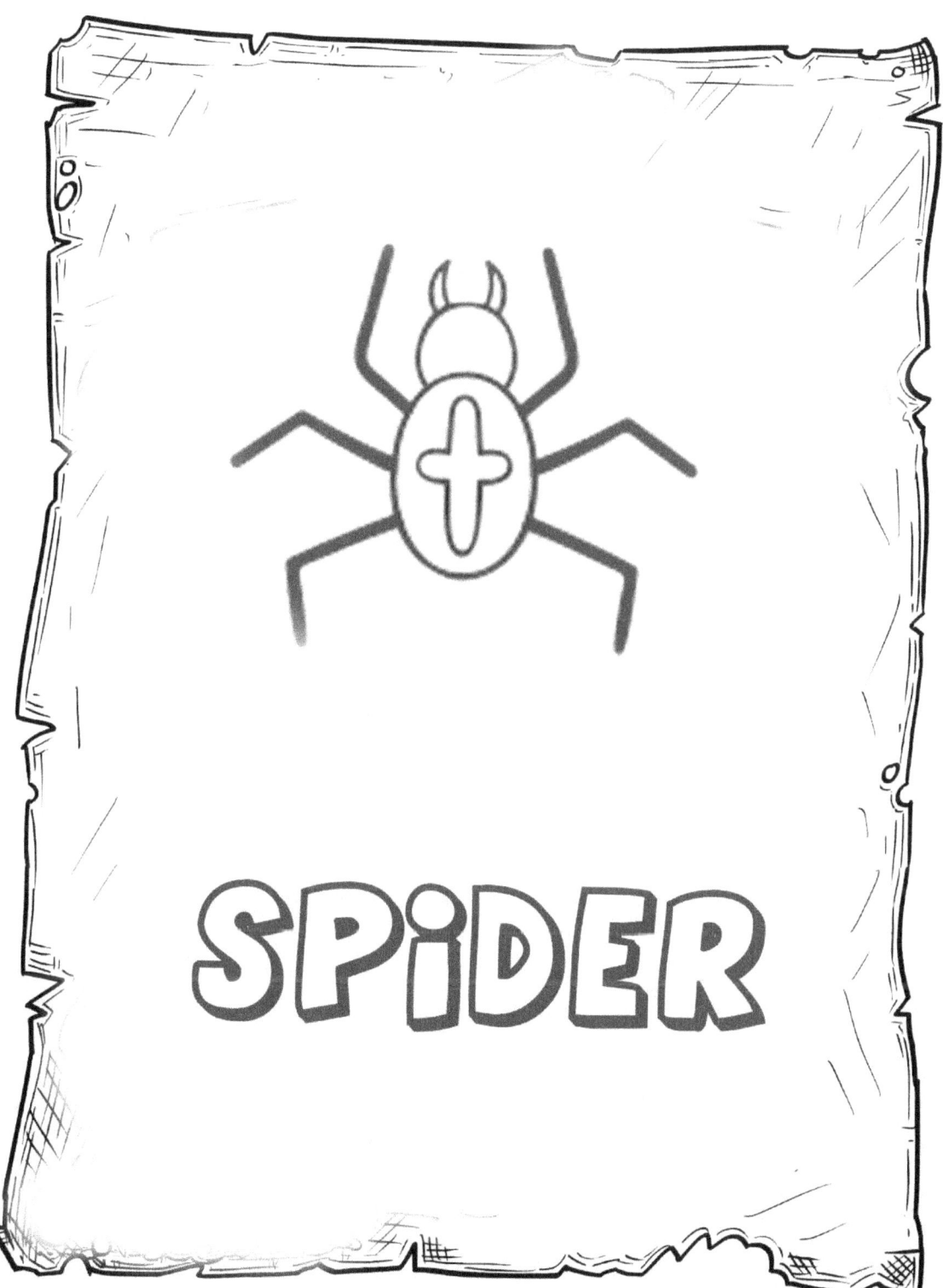

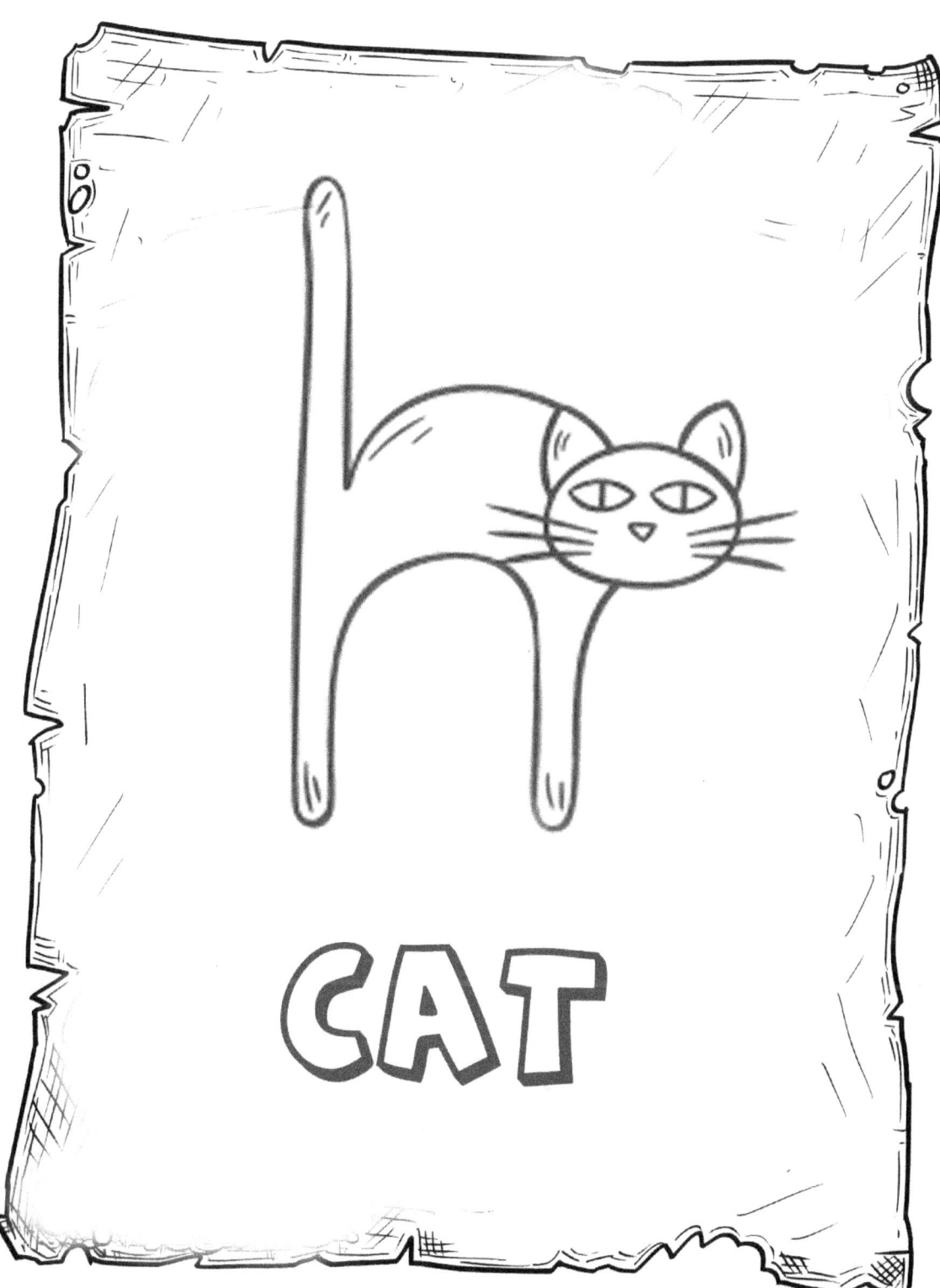

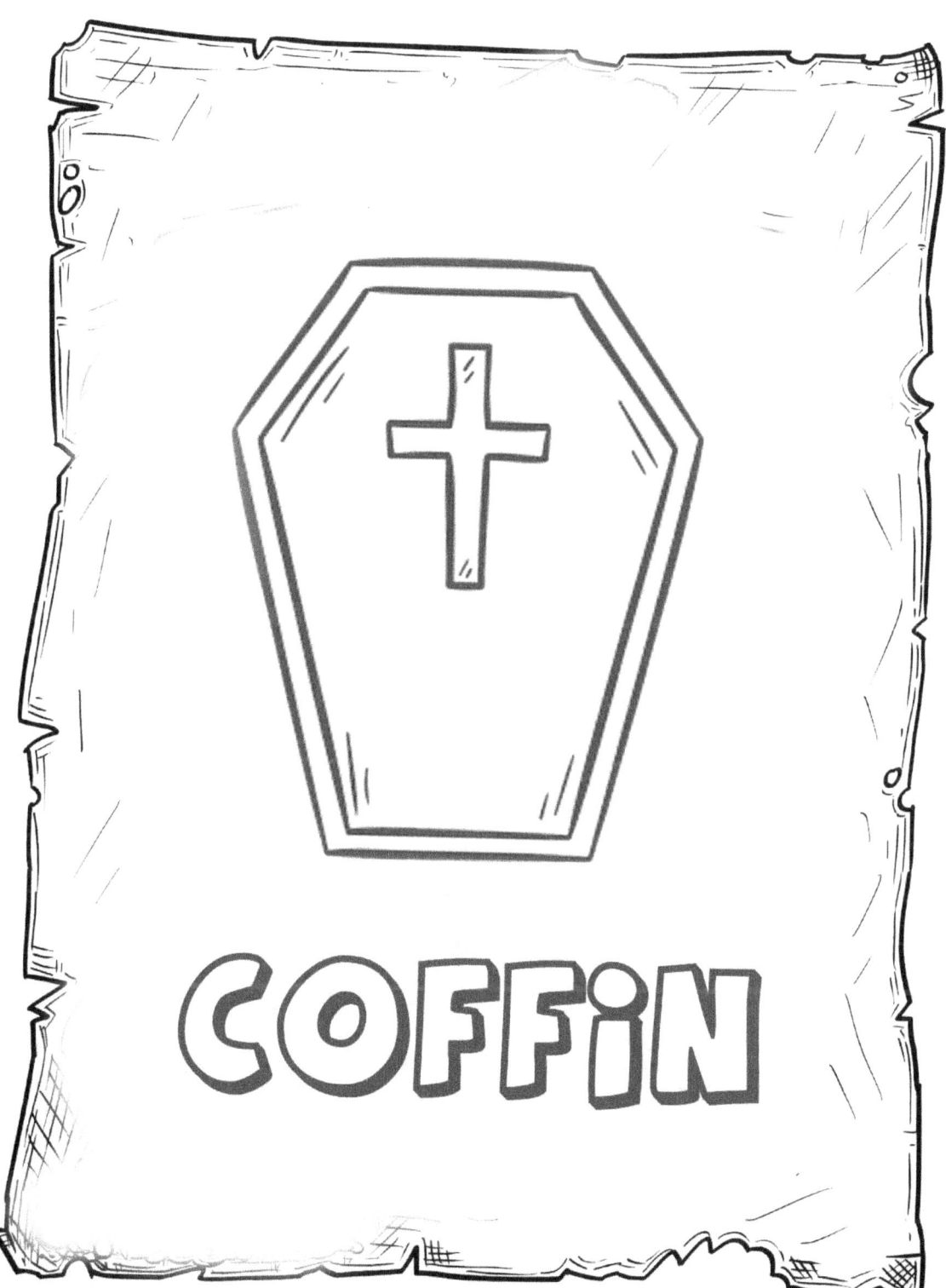

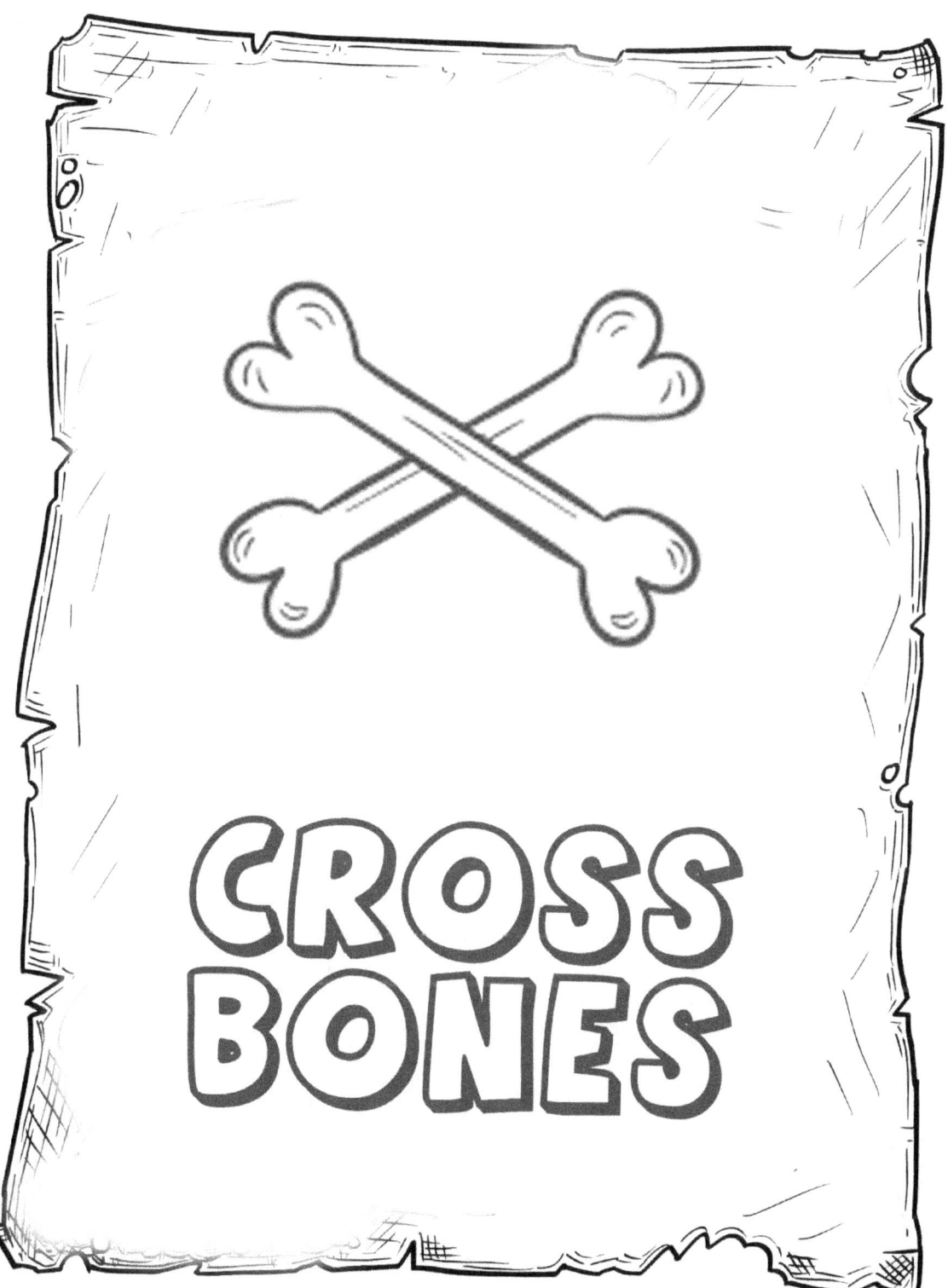

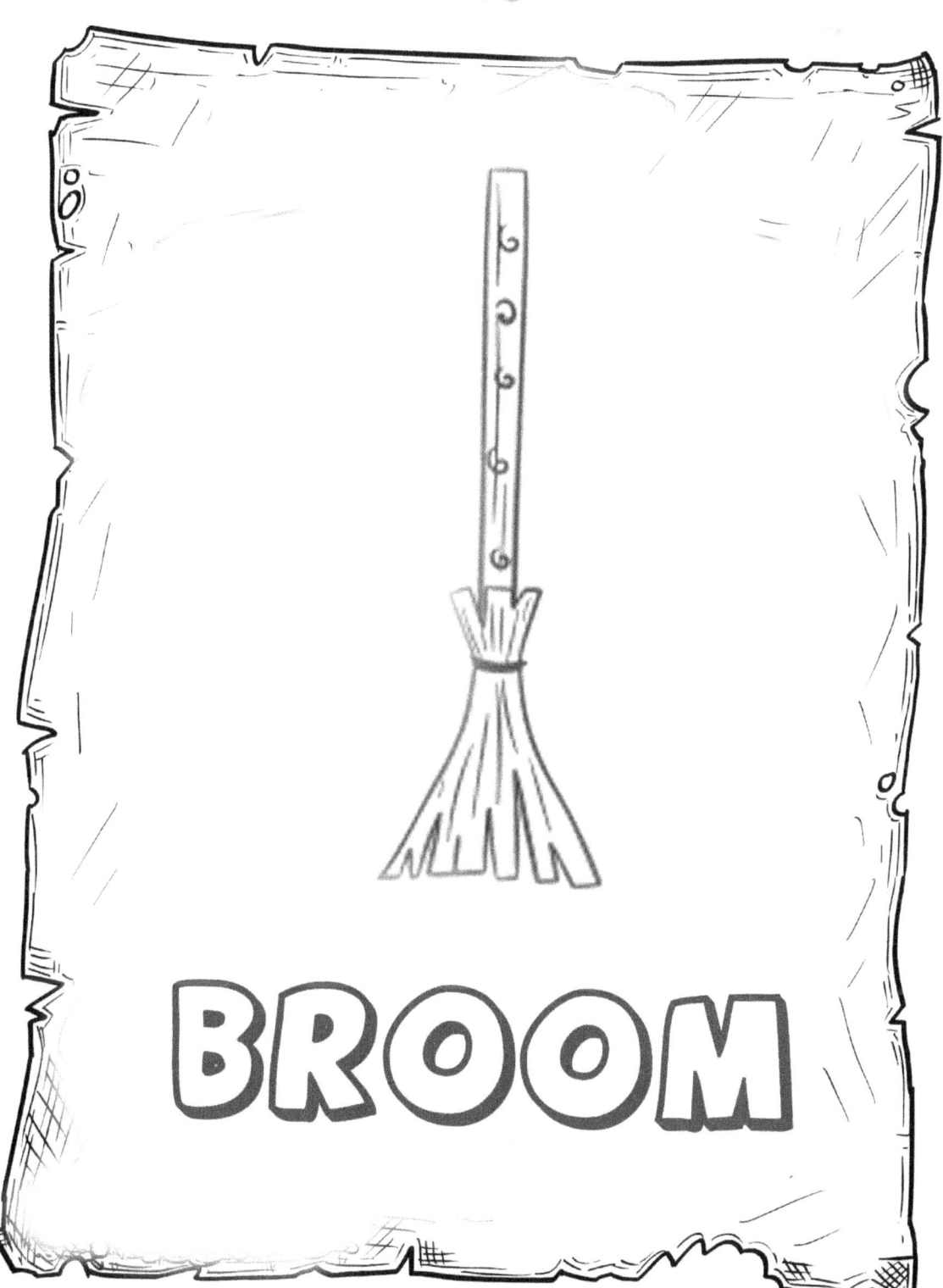

13 Words Halloween Coloring Book For Kids

(Dover Holiday Coloring Books)

"Practice Is The Best Way To Develop Skill"

Travis T. Johnson

www.ingramcontent.com/pod-product-compliance
Lightning Source LLC
Chambersburg PA
CBHW062209220526
45470CB00009B/2981